GOD IS STILL
SPEAKING TODAY

MARRIAGE MADE IN HEAVEN
(Ruth and Boaz of the 21st Century)

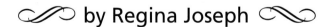 by Regina Joseph

 **REGINA JOSEPH**

My email is: *prophetessgina@live.co.uk*

My telephone number is: *07507238033*

For those who want to get in touch after reading this book, please contact me by phone, email or messenger.

God bless you

 **DEDICATION**

I dedicate this book to the Lord Almighty and pray that it will be used as a tool of encouragement and to stir up purpose in people's lives. I trust the Holy Spirit to help me to remember the dates and all the events that took place to make this book complete in Jesus' name.

✎ ACKNOWLEDGEMENTS ✎

I was inspired and quickened by the Spirit of God to write this book. I love and thank you, Holy Spirit, for your continual leading in my life.

My husband Bishop Peter Joseph for accepting me as God's will for your life. I love and thank God for you.

My maternal Grandmother, Monica Muzunze, 97 years of age. God has been good to you. We love and thank God for you.

Thank you to:

My Mother-in-law, Veronica Cossil Joseph and my late Father-in-law, Mr Nathaniel Colimbus Joseph, without you both my husband would not have been in this world.

My husband's siblings Thomas, Cathrine, Evette and Brian and their families, My husband's precious Children Joshua, Sheldon, Justin and his fiancée, Nadia his daughter and His Grand children Monique and Brook, and the entire Edgar family for accepting me into your family. I love you loads.

I remember my late Grandfather Lewis and my Grandmother Regina who raised us up and the sacrifices they made for us, and also whom my brother and I are named after. A big thank you to them both, we love and miss them.

I want to thank my precious Parents, Mum Olivia Muzunze, who went to be with the Lord. I miss her and love her loads and I know that she would have been proud of me.

To my Dad. I love you lots. For all the sacrifices you made thank you. You are a continual tower of strength to me and I am very proud to be called your daughter.

My precious Brother, Reverend Loui Benhura. I love you to bits. Nephew Noah. I love you.

To my younger Sister, Gamuchirai Mapira. I love you.

To all my Aunties, Carol, Rose, Pepe, Marjorie and all your husbands and children love you.

To the Benhura and Katsande Families all over the world.

I thank God for my late Dad's Sister Aunt Cathrine and her daughter Lucy who went to be with the Lord, we look forward to a reunion in God's timing. Aunt Cathrine also left behind Christine and Fungai, and as I write this book Christine is happily married to Augustine and they are blessed with 3 boys. Thank you guys for standing with us.

To Aunt Beatrice, Tino and all the Muzunze Families.

To the entire COLIM MINISTRIES who we oversee. My Husband, Bishop Peter Joseph, and I thank you for standing with us.

A big thank you to Evangelist George Williams, Evangelist Bernt Rosberg, Minister Anna Rosberg, and many others who came to confirm our Marriage.

To everyone who contributed to our wedding with any kind of service, contributed cash and gave precious time. I declare to you it was not in vain!

Thank you to Bishop Jos Brisette and Reverend Richard Mitchell for officiating at our wedding and we also honour and salute your wives.

Thank you to Pastors Colin and Amanda Dye, Kensington Temple City Church where God met me and convicted me.

Thank you to our Spiritual Covering and Parents in the Lord, Archbishop JP and Bishop Sodnaia Hackman from Trans Atlantic and Pacific Alliance of Churches.

Thank you to all who took part at our wedding,

The Entire bridal party at our wedding

The Catering team led Mother Verma Johnson

Decorating team led by Evangelist Pat Bennet

Minister Marva Laing, Reverend Hainsley Laing and Deaconess Margaret Wright.

The Sound and Media Crew

The Photography and Videography team

Mrs Winifred and Mr Chris Kargbo for the cake and transport

Apostle Isaac Ojok

Pastor Jeremiah and Pastor Elizabeth Emuchay

Pastor Cynthia Dixon

Pastor Isaac Mac Attram and Minister Sally who recently joined the family: we love and appreciate you both.

Pastor Caroline Joseph,

Pastor David and Pastor Naomi Midzi at Living Faith Temple Corby.

Pastor Cleto Mubwanda and his wife Sharon Mubwanda, Pastor Martin Keles and Pastor Adama Sesay

Thank you to our Friends and Associates that we met along the way:

Pastor Mel and Pastor Mavis Kabaso at Awake Grace Ministries International.

To all God send Mothers, Pastor Eileen Mutanhu, Minister Cresence Musunga and all the Watchman on the Wall team.

To Apostle William and Pastor Grace Munthali at Living Water Maidstone.

To Pastor John and Pastor Lovejoy Mpamela at Prayer without Ceasing and Bethel Dunamis Church.

To Pastor Tina Jones and Revive Ministry.

Pastor Audrey Francis at New Arc

Pastor Del and Carol Bearfoot

Apostle George and Pastor Anniete Sagbe

Pastor Joyce Vassel

Pastor Victor and Pastor Success Godwins

All Tapac Ministers, especially Bishop Anne my Bible School Tutor and Bishop Vanessa for your encouragement.

In case we forgot to mention your name, just remember you are valued and appreciated by God and by us too! Love you all and stay blessed!

 **FOREWORD**

A Word by my Husband Bishop Peter Joseph

I want to thank God for my African Bride, Prophetess and Reverend Regina Joseph. I love her very much and she holds a special place in my heart. I confirm that all she has said in this book is true and that is how it all happened. I also testify that ever since I married her my life has changed positively and many doors have opened to me. The Bible says *"He who finds a wife finds a good thing, and obtains favour from the Lord."* (Prov.18.22) Favour has truly been following me and I am very grateful to God for His plan for our lives. My wife is a gift for me from the Lord. I will continue to love her and cherish her. She has stood by my side through "thick and thin" for the last seven years and I know by God's grace and help we will grow old together in Jesus' name! I love you loads my First Lady!

A Word by Evangelist Bernt Rosberg from Norway

God gave me and my wife, Anna Rosberg, a word to confirm Bishop Peter and Prophetess Regina Joseph's marriage.

We left Bergen, Norway, to attend a Benny Hinn Conference in April 2008 at the ExCel Centre, when my wife and I met Bishop Peter Joseph with his fiancée, Prophetess Regina Joseph and two other church members who had come along with them. We met them at Greenwich Railway Station, London. We did not know naturally that they were a couple, but I remember my wife and I getting on the Docklands light railway and the moment we all sat, Anna my wife through instant divine revelation from God pointed out that Prophetess Regina Joseph was the Pastor's wife in the midst of two other women present. God had begun to speak to my wife the moment we got on the train. Indeed, by the time we got to the Benny Hinn conference God had downloaded a lot about this couple to me also. God revealed to me that He had put them together for the end time work of God.

I personally do not speak much English, so my wife had to interpret all that I was revealing to them and for that we are grateful to God. I confirm that the testimony in this book is true and it is to the glory of Jesus.

A Word by Pastor Isaac Mac Attram

God is in the business of putting marriages together. The decision to make Jesus your Lord and Saviour is the biggest and the most important decision anyone can make in life. Aside from our salvation, whom you marry is the next big decision. It is a decision that needs to be done carefully and prayerfully.

The testimony of bishop and prophetess's marriage is a testimony of heaven's choice and approving a couple to come together for His work. Prophetess had fasted and prayed for God to reveal her everything to do with her destiny and assignment. Up until this point Bishop was only a spiritual father to her, but I believe God who alone knows the hearts of men, had seen the faithfulness of them both in the ministry and decided to bless them both, by bringing them closer to each other as husband and wife. It was more like the Boaz and Ruth story replaying in our generation.

The announcement took many by surprise including myself as an associate Pastor of the church. I had travelled and on my return I was informed of what the Spirit of God had revealed to His maid servant, Prophetess Regina Joseph. I was not sure what to say at first but I had this inner witness and peace that if it was from the Lord, that he would confirm it in His time. We prayed for confirmation, and eventually God sent Prophet Bernt and his wife Anna Rosberg from Norway to confirm clearly that their union was from Him. Apart from them, many other ministers of God also came along to the ministry to confirm the same. May God be praised! However, many people in the ministry really struggled to believe or understand what God was doing with them and with the church at the time and some even left the fellowship. But with time it became very clear that God has called and chosen His servants for His work.

Today as I write this testimony, their marriage has now become a model marriage that all who know them look up to them, regarding the unity, commitment and love they exhibit towards each other. My prayer is that as you read this book, you will be encouraged to look to God and fast and pray about the one you should marry as that decision is not to be taken lightly. Your future partner is to be a destiny helper and not a destiny destroyer. Read this interesting story and may the Holy Spirit give you understanding.

God Bless you.

INTRODUCTION

by Author Regina Joseph nee Benhura

God is truly a Father to all of us and if we ask him and seek for His will and direction concerning any area of our life He will speak to us and lead us by His Spirit. Psalms 32:8 says *"I will instruct you and teach you in the way you should go; I will guide you with my eye"*. God desires to give us the best in everything. If our earthly father can shower us with good gifts, our Heavenly Father will give us the best. That is why it is important when it comes to any decision making to seek the counsel of God first in all things; it is especially important to have direction concerning the person you want to spend the rest of your life with. We can also seek counsel from ministers of God or other mature believers. The book of Proverbs says *"Trust in the Lord with all your heart, And lean not on your own understanding; In all your ways acknowledge Him, And He shall direct your paths."* (Prov: 3:5, 6) God knows who the perfect husband is for you so that you can complement each other. So to any single brother or sister reading about my testimony, let God lead you to and show you the right spouse.

We are living in a time where some marriages are not lasting due to so many factors. For example, making a wrong choice of spouse by going for looks or material things rather than a person's heart or character; lack of communication and negligence; financial challenges; unresolved conflicts; adultery; the list is endless. Nowadays couples find it hard to commit to one another. There are so many temptations and if one is not God-fearing, nor has the fruit of self-control they will give in. There are also demonic forces that are sent from hell to frustrate marriage, especially Christian marriages. If we are not very prayerful or are not united we give the devil an opportunity to bring disorder into our marriages.

As you read this book you will discover that God deals with all of us on an individual basis, depending on our purpose, assignment and destiny. God's ways are not our ways and neither are His thoughts our thoughts. The more willing we are to be yielded vessels to Him the more we can experience His hand of blessing. Join me now as I take you as far as my childhood. How this journey began…

CONTENTS

Humble Beginnings

God is amazing! Whoever would have thought that I, Regina Joseph nee Benhura, would end up in the United Kingdom married to a servant of God and I too also preaching and prophesying to nations?

All I can say is that this can only be the doing and arrangement of our Almighty sovereign God and my earthly father who was instrumental in the process. God knew exactly before I was born my end from the beginning.

The book of Jeremiah confirms this by saying, *"Before I formed you in the womb I knew you; Before you were born I sanctified you; I ordained you a prophet to the nations."* (Jer.1:5)

Only God knew about this, even before I was in my mother's womb. In God's eyes and mind my life was already structured and planned. All that was left was the physical manifestation of what was in God's heart. And now I have come to understand that God will do anything to make sure the plans He has concerning our lives come to pass.

I was born in Mutoko and I grew up in the capital of Zimbabwe, Harare. My parents gave birth to my brother Loui and I when they were young and not so mature. Unfortunately they later divorced. My brother and I were like twins. We both used to have similar interests, climbing fruit trees and running around all over our garden. We got on so well with each other and also with all our other cousins Christine, Michelle, Fungai and the other little ones who were born much later than us. Around the age of five our grandparents became our legal guardians along with my father. They looked after us and our

Mum would also come and take us to spend quality time with her. Our Dad used to take my brother and I to jazz festivals and theme parks in our local town.

During that period in our lives a door of opportunity opened for my father to come to England. When he left for England our grandparents then did their best to raise us in the way of the Lord. We were raised in the Catholic faith and prayed every night as a family and fasted during Lent. We attended a service every Sunday called Mass in Catholicism. We had Christian values instilled in us from childhood. We were taught Christian morals and discipline and the fear of God. I remember going to St Francis Church in Waterfalls every Sunday and being a very active member, especially in singing and sometimes teaching Sunday school. I even once or twice had an opportunity to visit people suffering from AIDS and I had the privilege to listen to their testimonies and encourage them in prayer and the Word of God. From that time I developed more compassion and until today that compassion has increased. I try my best to help in any way I can to relieve the suffering of others from time to time.

Why Me?

In primary school I did not feel I could fit in with the others very well; I was very timid but intelligent. I used to be bullied but I could not share it with anyone. I was even taken advantage of many times by the girl whose father used to rent a few rooms in our properties. I even acted it out as I got so confused and messed up in my mind but no one knew except me and God. At home I was different; I acted all strong and was very talkative. I was only an introvert when it to came to sensitive issues of the heart. The bullying even came from my teacher. No matter how good my grades were, for this woman I was never good enough. I remember we used to play about and match each other with the boys in our school in a joking way, but one day it was taken out of context and became a big issue. One day someone decided to be crafty and they matched me with a certain boy in my absence. The worst thing was that our names were written on the blackboard where everyone could see.

There was jeering and screaming and applauding in the class due to that incident so our tutor who had attended a staff meeting had to hurry back to see what the noise was all about. When she found out my name was written on the blackboard she boiled with anger, I was later told. I had joined the Girl Scouts a year before so when all this happened I was absent from the classroom. When I came back my tutor embarrassed me, announcing in front of the whole class that at our next school assembly two days later she was going to announce how I was more involved in boys than in education. I was shocked and fear got the better of me. All my intimidators were cheering, but before I could catch my breath the school bell rang to signal the end of day. How could I defend myself?

I took my school bag and walked home in so much fear and confusion. Why was I hated like this? What crime had I committed? Nothing happened really between us and the boys. There was no relationship so what was the big deal? A strong thought came into my mind to attempt suicide. I felt it was better to die than suffer shame. I used to hear of stories of people drinking poison and throwing themselves over the bridge, but I knew I was not bold enough to do that. My grandmother and aunt were nurses so there were always tablets in our medicine cupboard. I began to plan what I was going to do. I was afraid to tell anyone what I was going through so I decided to keep it to myself. I wrote a note of how I wished I was dead and hid it but it was later found and I was questioned about it.

The following morning I sneaked into our medicine cupboard, being careful not to be caught in the process, and I managed to be successful and not a soul heard my footsteps. Thank God, I thought to myself. I carried a plastic cup in which I was to collect water from the tap at school and put it in my school bag. The story continued in our classroom but things seemed much calmer that day than the day before. When the bell rang for the end of the day that Tuesday afternoon I sped to the toilet, quickly got water from the tap, walked quickly out of the school yard and started overdosing myself with different tablets. I took approximately 35 different kinds of tablets, to the extent that by the time I got home I was acting like a drunken girl. As the tablets began to take effect on my body my Auntie Marjorie, who is now a Deaconess in our church, noticed me unstable on my knees and I revealed to her what I had done.

Immediately an ambulance was called and I ended up at Harare Central Hospital. That night I was drained with a tube and most of the tablets I had consumed came out. It is truly a miracle that I am alive today. I was moments away from death but God used the hand of the medical staff to revive me back to life. The whole family was devastated. They could not understand what I was going through. My other Auntie, Pee, short for Pepe, consoled me and tried to find out the root cause of this incident but I decided not to speak. I acted stubbornly but inside I was shattered and upset that I had survived. Why did I not die? Why did God preserve my life? I did get angry with God at that time, asking why He had not allowed me to have my own way. I did not find those answers then but now I know God had great plans for me.

My father in England was informed. My mother came over to take us away on holiday. The entire extended family was informed but not many had the boldness to question my behaviour. My Dad called and we spoke but he did not have many words to say to me. He encouraged me that whatever the reason I had done it, all would be sorted out and I just agreed with him. I had acted out of pain, fear and rejection at school. I wanted to be loved by my teacher and my peers but I seemed to be nothing at all to some people. My grandparents died much later without even knowing why I had attempted suicide. They had been deeply affected and hurt.

Even when Mum took us on holiday she was upset first with herself; she most probably blamed her absence in our home for my reckless behaviour. She was upset with me so she questioned me but I did not give an accurate answer. Instead I told a lie which made no sense whatsoever. I was a mystery to my Mum.

Even up to her death she never understood why I decided to end my life. But one thing I know is that my Mum loved me dearly and as the first born child she expected me to lead by example to my younger brother. Mum was fair skinned and had long Afro hair with jerry curls. Many people tell me even today that I am the spitting image of her, even including my mannerisms and my taste for very nice things, because she too was like that. I also resemble my paternal and maternal Grandmother.

My Maternal Grandmother Monica Muzunze is 97 years of age and God has kept her to this point! We used to visit her a lot in Mutoko, when we were much younger. That visit was also a time of building relationships with my entire Mum's family who lived with Grandma. Mutoko was quite a long bus ride away, but despite the distance, it gave us an opportunity to view the country side more.

Whenever my brother and I went over to visit her she would ask the helpers in her farm to slaughter a goat and chickens for us. We would have a barbeque and had a time of great feasting and catching up with all of them…

New Start

After the attempted suicide episode people were more careful around me. It was like having "Big Brother" filming in the house. I was being watched in every detail as they did not want a repeat of the previous time. If I did fall ill I was thoroughly supervised to make sure I took the correct amount of tablets. We continued with life as if nothing had happened. At school everything eventually died down.

Despite all that I had been through I continued going to church most Sundays. I really enjoyed meeting all kinds of people at church, especially the Nuns in the church monastery. I came to a point where I felt I wanted to be a Nun myself. This meant dedicating my life totally to God with no chance of getting married or having children. I felt that lifestyle suited me better but when I look back I realised it was my hunger and passion for God at an early age that was the driving force but I did not understand the price I had to pay. I do not speak against anyone who is called to be a Nun because God has different plans for every individual. In fact I salute and respect those who are fervently called by God to be single, as Apostle Paul was, to serve Him with no spouse helping to share the burden.

When the Nuns in our church held events or open days I would visit them. During my school holidays I started visiting various monasteries. My heart was set on it but after a lot of wise counsel from grandparents I decided not to join the Nuns. My grandparents pointed out firstly how young I was and the commitment and sacrifice involved in being a Nun. They even asked me if I really understood what this was really about. I was convinced and decided to wait till I was much older but by the time I became older I had changed my mind. This truly showed that my grandparents were correct to make me understand that I was not yet mature enough to make life changing decisions.

I have always had a hunger for God and most of my family back in Zimbabwe know. We would go to any gathering to do with God, if we were allowed. When I heard there were crusades in town I would ask for permission to go. There was no doubt that God had called me. I remember one day in our church there was a group of men and women from another local town who used to hold Catholic Charismatic renewal meetings. I started attending those and even meetings in our local town where Christians from all backgrounds met.

I went to a single sex girls' high school and was involved there in the Christian Union, where girls from various denominations met to hear the Word and to praise and worship God. I would lead praise and worship and share with my fellow sisters. Between 1995 and 1996 I gave my life to God but I was still not truly converted and convicted. Between 1997 and 1999 it was a period of great mourning for me. My grandfather, my aunt (Dad's sister) and my mother all died during this period. I was really down and I really needed great encouragement. By this time I had already finished secondary school.

During this period I met a young man who liked me and whom I later liked too. He was a friend and encourager, especially as I was still mourning. I did not know then what the future held, so we dated for a year; but around the time we were dating arrangements were made for me to come to England. I left him in Zimbabwe, travelled to England and tried to stay in touch but it was not easy to maintain a long distance relationship on the phone. I even made attempts to bring him over but the door never opened, and I as I look back it was not in God's will to do so. It is very important to include this information so that you can understand where I came from and how I ended up with my husband today.

Life in the UK

When I arrived in the UK I did not know what exactly God had planned for me, so in my first year in the United Kingdom which was year 2000, I attended Greenwich Community College. I had the privilege of studying AS Levels in English and also a Vocational Course in Health and Social Care. I later also attended South Chelsea College to study a Course in Business Studies.

In the same year that I was at Greenwich College, I met my step-daughter, Nadia Joseph, who is presently the only daughter of my husband. This will shock many people but it is the truth. I even attended some lectures with her in the same class. I never knew I would end up being married to her father, Bishop Peter Joseph.

In that college I also had the privilege of meeting Lennette Randall, who I later found out was to become my destiny connector. Lennette was a born again Christian on fire for God. She is the one who introduced me to the Christian Union in Greenwich College and I later found out that she too was a very close friend of Nadia Joseph my step-daughter.

I thank God for Lennette Randall for the part she has played in my life. She is also the one who connected me to the church where I later found the Pastor who was destined to be my husband. God knew Lennette was my destiny connector. Why I say that is because a year later I left Greenwich College and there was a time when we lost touch completely. However, no matter where we both went, God caused us to meet again and again!

As for the relationships arena, I did date men when I first arrived in the United Kingdom. My earnest heart's desire was to settle down in marriage with the first person I met, but unfortunately the culture here was shocking for me. I did not meet anyone who was in agreement with my values at all. Once you date someone for a while the next thing was to have physical intimacy. I was really disappointed then, but because I was not totally in submission to God, I accepted dates from wrong men who rejoiced in defiling women and treating women like they had no value!

The devil even sent my way a young man who I ended up going out with. At that time that man introduced me to clubbing. We used to go out clubbing every other Saturday and some Sundays I would go for the Catholic Church Service which is called Mass. I had no conviction at all! God loves me honestly! I even used to listen to worldly music and was even introduced to drinking strong spirit drinks and wine. I never really got drunk and God preserved me even in that club. Many times I would hear this one was stabbed in that club, but as for me God knew my end so I was safe in his merciful Father's arms despite my sin and state.

When I look back now I realise the Annointing upon my life was the devil's target. I did not understand what I carried inside so therefore I was easy prey. But God remained faithful through it all and did surprise me later on...

God Knows Best...

At the same time I came to the United Kingdom, my paternal grandmother Regina Benhura nee Katsande came to live with us from Zimbabwe. We were overjoyed to have her around, but unfortunately she fell ill and went to be with the Lord in April 2004. I had looked up to her in so many ways and now she was gone. I was still in a grieving period, as it was not long since I had lost my Mum and other loved ones too. What a season I was passing through !

In that same year I moved to Northolt West London from Thamesmead South. I also lost a university opportunity due to settlement issues at this time and I was very disappointed. It seemed to me everything was falling apart around me, but little did I know but that *"my redemption drew near"* (Lk.21:28).

My Secondary school friend from Zimbabwe, Makafunga Senderayi had been born again for a while and she was attending Kensington Temple City Church in Notting Hill Gate in London. She invited me so many times to her church but I had refused on the basis that I was born a Catholic and I would die a Catholic, and that truly she had no power to convert me. So when everything started going wrong in my life and I was at the crossroads where I did not really know where to turn, I decided to give my Friend Maka a call and ask the directions to her church. She was shocked about my call because of my previous attitude, but I later found out she and another friend called Fifi Mokwana and some members of Maka's prayer group had been praying for me to be fully committed to God. The strange thing is, prior to all this, I had started ministering and praying for a friend of mine called

Maya. I still visited clubs in my pain to try and get around all that I was going through, but the amazing thing is that during my last visit there, I felt I could not fit or belong there anymore. Tears streamed down my cheeks as I was in the club. I really wondered why I was there in the first place. I had a new perspective of things all of a sudden. God was surely doing something to me. I would later find out what it was.

During this period I decided to call upon God with all my heart. In December 2005 I rededicated my life at Kensington Temple in Notting Hill Gate. When I look back this was truly my born again experience. My life quickly began to transform. I was baptised in water and was later baptised in the Holy Spirit.

From then on it was as if I had received another zest of life. Such inner joy, strength and determination entered into my inner being and I was truly a new creation to the glory of His name. From that day onwards I sought God like a hungry baby seeking its mother's milk. I prayed, read the Word and praised God like never before. By 2006 I was even praying and hearing from God.

In Notholt I was living with my Aunt Rose, my Dad's sister, and her husband, Uncle Ed, his sister Chiga and their three children. The transformation that took place in my life also had an effect on my aunt and family, so that they too gave their lives to Jesus. My Aunt Rose is now a Deaconess and my uncle an elder in their local church.

Between 2004 and 2006 whilst I was living with Uncle Ed and Auntie Rose I helped them with baby-sitting, at the same time teaching the children about God, looking after the home and doing all the chores while they were at work. I treated those children like my own and the house as if it were mine. I am also convinced this is also why two years later God saw my heart towards my aunt and uncle's children and the way I treated their home and decided to speed up my blessing of a husband from the Lord.

My experience reminds me a lot about the story of Esther in the Bible.

Esther was prepared to meet with her husband with the help of Hegai the Eunuch. I knew some day I would get married but I did not know when. Living with my aunt and uncle helped me to gain the experience I needed later on about running a home. The following verse describes the kind of preparation Esther had to go through before she was presented before the king.

"Each young woman's turn came to go in to King Ahasuerus after she had completed twelve months' preparation, according to the regulations for the women, for thus were the days of their preparation apportioned: six months with oil of myrrh, and six months with perfumes and preparations for beautifying women" (Esther 2:12). Even though God is not mentioned in the above Scripture of preparation for Esther, I have now come to understand that God takes preparation seriously for any assignment He has

for us. So He will even allow everyday situations and tasks to mould us to be what He wants us to be some day.

In October 2006 I left my aunt's home because I felt it was time to follow my calling. I knew God had called me to be a prophet because of the prophecy I had received that God had called me like Jeremiah to be a prophet to the nations. I used to pray for people and I would receive supernatural revelation concerning people's lives, and it happened to be true when I inquired of them individually.

When I moved from Northolt I came back to Thamesmead, South East London, to live with my father. By then it was the end of October 2006 and I was preparing to begin Bible School. I was praying and trusting God to make a way financially for me. My heart was truly set on Kensington Temple Church Bible School. I wanted to be thoroughly equipped for my calling so I was willing to make the sacrifice. Having moved back to the South East, I realised the distance was going to be too great to go to my church.

A few days after coming back home I decided to contact Lennette Randall, who I have already mentioned I had felt strongly was sent by God for me as a connector to destiny. I explained my plans to Lennette and she suggested that I could visit one of the Wednesday Fire meetings at the "Sanctuary". She told me that Nadia Joseph's dad, Peter Joseph, who is now my husband, was running those meetings in Plumstead.

I hesitated because at Kensington Temple we had experienced the fire and presence of God and I honestly wanted to attend meetings that were similar to those at my church. After Lennette's gentle persuasion I decided to accompany her one Wednesday and the moment I walked into the Sanctuary God met me there. The man of God prophesied to me about my calling and the exact words he said were: I had found favour in the sight of God like Esther. With such confirmation I attended every Wednesday and still went to my church in Notting Hill Gate.

I later found out there was an ongoing School of Ministry class in the Sanctuary. Because it was near I enrolled and whilst

I was in the class God began to speak to me more. Apostle Peter Joseph prayed for me and started showing me how to fast effectively with results. He also took me through deliverance so God could do a deep work in me. He taught me a lot of spiritual things and whenever he taught me the Spirit of God would confirm it to me at home. From then on the Spirit of God started nudging me about going on long fasts.

∽ A Year Later... ∾

I had been praying and asking God for direction concerning my life in prayer since I rededicated my life to Jesus back in 2005. I did not want to do things my own way; I wanted God to bring enlightenment. As I was fasting I would wait upon the Lord, sometimes listening to praise and worship, and even being quiet and still meditating on God's goodness.

One night in October 2007 I had no agenda whatsoever and had no clue that this was to be my Encounter Night. It was an ordinary night. Nothing special was happening but God chose that night to reveal to me something that was not in my mind at all. All that I wanted was to spend quality time and enjoy His sweet presence. For me this was my "honeymoon period" with God. As I had been waiting upon Him for a while, I heard the Spirit of God speaking clearly to my spirit, saying "Peter Joseph is your husband." It was a still small voice at that time. The Bible says, *"The sheep follow him, for they know his voice. Yet they will by no means follow a stranger."* (Jn.10:4,5). So who was speaking?

This was not the first time I had heard the Holy Spirit speak but the statement He had mentioned surprised me. The man to whom the Spirit of God was referring was my Pastor. I had not asked God for a husband lately so I wondered what this was all about that I was hearing in my spirit.

I had prayed a prayer a year or two earlier specifying the husband I would like but my Pastor did not fit all the description. I was in a season where all my satisfaction came from ministering to the Lord and serving him so marriage was not in the picture.

I responded to the Spirit of God with a loud voice, "No way Lord! He is too old!" I respected my Pastor and his hunger and passion for the things of God. I used to see him and still do today as a role model. We were not courting or in any relationship that would lead to marriage, so when I heard the voice of God speak to my spirit it was not at all what I was expecting. That night I did struggle a bit to get to sleep because I was beginning to doubt if it was truly the voice of God or my own desires. A few days later I decided to confide in a brother who I know is strong in God and is a seasoned prophet.

The Bible says in Proverbs 15:22: *"Without counsel, plans go awry, but in the multitude of counsellors they are established."* This information had deeply troubled me so I called him on the phone. I knew this brother hears God accurately because many times he had given a prophecy and it was very accurate. He also knew the Word of God. I just told the brother what God had told me concerning my Pastor. The brother then advised me to ask God for clarity. I was very grateful for his counsel and I did ask God as directed.

The Bible tells us that we should test every spirit, so to make sure that it was really God who spoke to me, I started praying prophetically asking God for confirmation. This was roughly towards the end of October 2007. My prayer point was that if God had truly spoken He should send confirmation and that if it was the enemy then the door would be shut immediately. The year 2007 ended but I did not hear anything at all to do with what God had told me before. I thought to myself it must have been a crazy idea, I had in my head.

As 2008 began I was excited about the new things God had for us as a Ministry. I felt a strong nudge to do more fasting and prayer. I had really kept what I heard from the Spirit of God the previous year as a secret. I never told my Pastor when the Lord spoke to me for the first time about him. I just continued with my life as if I had never heard anything from God. I sensed in my spirit that it was a forty day fast that I was required to do. I did not enjoy fasting because we fasted three days a week already, so a longer fast meant not eating that much at all. But fasting to me spiritually was great and it would catapult me deep into the things of God. Also, because I had fasted for longer periods before and had seen God's hand move mightily upon my life I chose to give it a go again.

The fourteenth day of my fasting was 14 January 2008. I was lying on my bed at my Aunt Pepe's house in Gravesend. It was a very cold January morning and due to the fasting I was very weak and decided just to worship God in my heart. It was before midday and I felt a bit sleepy due to the warmth of the heater. Suddenly I heard the Spirit of God speak to me in a strong and firm voice saying, "I have chosen Peter Joseph to be your husband and you shall be like Ruth and Boaz; call him and tell him now." Oh, wow, so this was God? He had spoken nearly two months earlier and was now clarifying to me that I had heard from him before. This instruction was not to be joked with. I did not laugh because I sensed the seriousness in the voice of the Spirit of God. I just said "Ruth and Boaz, oh it's been a while since I read the book of Ruth."

I was shocked so I decided to take my blanket and cover my face. The instruction God had given me was too tough and more like a command. I could not tell a man, least of all my Pastor, that information, so my carnal nature tried to fight God's instruction. But there was no way God was going to allow my flesh to get in the way of what He wanted to do with me. I was in denial!

In my heart I thought I would not obey this commanding voice. I really fought from within my heart and all the little strength within me. For me I just wanted to sleep and not wake up. But no matter how I tried to sleep, the Spirit of God supernaturally suspended my sleep and I became fully awake with no desire whatsoever to sleep.

I thought to myself "Why is God doing this to me? Is He trying to embarrass me?" The unusual thing is that when I had moved in with my Auntie Pepe and Uncle Robert's house in Gravesend with their two daughters in January 2008, God started dealing with me about ironing the family laundry. During that time I helped with laundry and house chores. There were five of us in the house including me but the Spirit of the Lord especially led me to iron men's trousers. I personally do not enjoy ironing; I just obeyed as a child of God. When I was ironing those trousers it was as if a hand were guiding me. I would put out my girl cousins' clothes to iron but the Lord continued to lead me to iron the male trousers and shirts first and everything else afterwards. When I think about it now it seems that the idea was for me to improve my ironing skills.

When my sleep had been suspended I then called my Pastor straight away to inform him what the Lord had told me and at that moment I told him on the phone. He reprimanded me, asking how I could tell him such information on the phone! I later made an appointment to meet him and shared with him what the Spirit of God had told me. He was shocked and surprised but all he said to me was that He did not doubt the Lord had spoken to me but at that time when I presented that information to Him, He was not aware. I just decided to wait and see what would happen but deep inside I was confused by his statement.

The way God had revealed it to me first and not to my husband brought to my mind the story of how the Angel Gabriel approached Mary first and not Joseph to announce the divine conception of our Lord Jesus Christ. Such situations are not easy to deal with and in normal daily life it is unheard of. I was a new creation and the ways of God were in no way similar to the ways of humans. I sensed strongly it was a time to truly ask God for the mind of Christ because all I was passing through was not humanly making any sense. If the messenger of God had not confirmed to Joseph about Mary, then he would have quietly ended the relationship to avoid her being judged or despised, considering they were about to marry. What was going to happen to me?

A sense of guilt and regret came over me. What on earth had I done by obeying the voice of God? If it was another big mistake what was going to happen to me? I continued fasting and I lost a lot of weight because of thinking too much as well. I had never been through anything like this in my life. Neither had I heard of anything like that before. There were not many people I could identify with concerning this situation. So I waited…

Those who Wait upon the Lord
shall Renew their Strength

In my time of waiting God gave me peace. A week after I had informed my Pastor God confirmed to him that He had given him a Flower in his garden. With that information we decided to share with others, though at this stage the testimony was only developing.

Hope was stirred again in me; at least something was unfolding but the thought of being with a man twenty-five years older than me haunted me a bit. I thought to myself, he has white hair and what would people say? He had a youthful body but he was still more mature than me by far in all areas. What would my father and the rest of the family say? They had known my Pastor as a shepherd. Now he was to be a son-in-law. My Pastor, on the other hand, was battling with similar issues of marrying a younger woman and also wondering what the reaction of the people would be when they found out. I broke the silence by telling my father directly. In Zimbabwean culture you were not supposed to tell your father directly; one needed a go-between person, such as an aunt like my Dad's sister, to stand in the gap for me on issues regarding marriage.

My father was shocked and did not say much to me. We spoke of other things and then left his place, but the truth was that I did not know what was going on in his mind after giving him such news. I called my aunts and I could also sense from their tone of voice that they did not know what else to say to me. The family I come from love me dearly and are very protective and so is my husband's family. For my family his age was not the issue, but it was the "God said" part they did not understand. Honestly, if it was new for me it was new for them too. My Pastor announced to the elders and members of the church what the Lord had said and many people were upset that day. Some walked out and even to this day have never returned. Some of our family who were also in the Ministry were hurt by the news and they too left as they did not understand. But now, years later, we are seeing the hand of God moving mightily upon our lives. Some of the youth in the Ministry at that time thought it was a set-up and some of them fought back with backbiting and gossip. I had to hold my peace or else I would have had a breakdown. God's grace sustained me throughout this period. It was His will for me to go through this so after I received my blessing we would value each other and we would have been refined in different ways.

We went to men and women of God who had been Pastors for years, for counsel and prayers but once we revealed what the Spirit of God had said they were challenged by the fact that God had spoken to me first. They had never come across such a story in their entire lives as believers. One particular man of God questioned us both to the extent that by the time we left his office my head was beginning to pound. He told us that he did not doubt my story but that the age difference was something that bothered him. This servant of God we saw was worried about the physical changes that take place in the body as people age. His main concern was that when my husband became elderly I would still be in my prime and he wondered how I would cope with the demands of physical intimacy because he reckoned that research shows that couples who are far apart in age experience such problems. I had honestly thought all those things through but I was standing on the word God had given. Heaven had chosen a spouse for me, so

I had to trust that the same God who spoke would make a way. The counsel was very wise as we listened to it but in my case God had spoken. Was God a liar or did human beings not understand God's will for us????

We left that particular man of God's office in such a state and in great silence but we took on board all that he had said to us.

We continued to pray and trust God for more confirmation. We had to continue to stand on the Word of God that says in Jeremiah 29:11, *"For I know the thoughts that I think toward you, says the Lord, thoughts of peace and not of evil, to give you a future and a hope."*

My Pastor had been married before but unfortunately the marriage had broken down. God had blessed him with three lovely sons and a daughter and now two granddaughters. After the marriage broke down he kept on trusting God to repair the marriage but unfortunately it did not work out. As a man he could not stay single unless he were to commit to being single for the rest of his life. To be practical and truthful, it is difficult if one has been married before to stay single unless it is God's will.

After the marriage broke down God gave him a powerful ministry of prayer, healing, deliverance and signs and wonders. In that ministry many Pastors came from all over to pray, to have fellowship and to be encouraged. So many great testimonies of healing and deliverance took place in people's lives over the years. That is why my friend Lennette Randall had introduced me to him when I had moved from Northolt back to Thamesmead. It was because of what God was doing through his ministry.

One day, out of principle, we had a discussion with my Pastor about the importance of making an appointment with his ex-wife to make her aware of what God had said to me about me being his wife. His ex-wife agreed and we went there. Present in the house that day was my step–daughter Nadia, her Mum and her aunt, her Mum's sister. My Pastor said to his ex-wife that even though God had spoken to me he was still willing to be with her if she was willing to take him back. The ex-wife refused on the basis that she had no desire to be a Pastor's wife, come what may. She and her sister questioned me thoroughly. They too said they were not in agreement with my story. I could sense they were not sure about my motives, which to me was quite natural, especially since my Pastor was the father of her children. I respect my husband's ex-wife because even though their marriage had not worked out she still wanted what was best for my Pastor. The good thing is we left her house with peace knowing we had done all that was humanly possible to inform her and also get her permission and to show her respect. I was happy because everything was in the open. So it was now left for God to do the rest.

May the God of heaven be praised!

Throughout this process we were passing through, we both had good days and bad days. There were days when we were so confident and happy but there were also days when we were really low. God dealt with us both individually and corporately, because the transition from him being my shepherd and mentor to being my husband involved a lot of changes on his part.

God putting us together meant we were going to be walking and working hand in hand. I have to say God remained faithful throughout this period, upholding us, keeping us safe and strengthening us daily.

In the midst of all this we prayed specific prayer points to God.

1. We said to God that if it had really been He who had spoken to me then would He please send a couple our way who had gone through a similar experience to ourselves and who also had such a wide gap in age so that we could identify with them.

2. We specifically asked God to choose a couple from outside the United Kingdom, as that way it would be more authentic and respectable to those who would hear about us.

My Pastor and I, my Aunt Marjorie and another girl fasted with us together for twenty-one days. During that time I was now living with Aunt Marj and another precious sister in the Lord, Norma. We prayed together every day and night to know God's way. We fasted for twenty-one days and God answered. I have to honestly say I ended my fast hours earlier than everyone else as the enemy was frustrating me, telling me I was wasting my time.

But as God would have it, and He being a father, He sent answers to our prayers and sacrifice. God knows how much we can all bear so the following Monday an Apostle came with a word from the Lord saying, "Do not lust after the girls in the church; marry one of them." The church often has more women than men and our ministry team also had more women than men. At this time my Pastor was also beginning to have doubts. He was having a 'yo-yo' attitude, which meant that he accepted God's will but when he counted the cost of all that we were going through he felt like giving up. I nearly tried to take my life again but God delivered me.

That same week, on the Wednesday, an Evangelist called George walked into the church. I was lying behind the altar soaking in the presence of God. The moment he walked in he started prophesying, saying "The Lord said I have given you a young wife; you shall be like Ruth and Boaz." He also said "Your wife will not come with anything, but accept her." At that moment I felt like God was in the room. My Pastor was shocked as these were the same exact words the Lord had told me. My spirit got so excited that even my physical body responded with joy. This man had no natural knowledge of what God had said to me and neither had we told him so I knew it was straight from heaven. My Pastor was now more convinced and he decided to ask for my hand in marriage at one of our Wednesday services. The exact word God gave me was said so I knew I really had heard from God without a doubt.

Who were Ruth and Boaz?
Ruth chapter 1-4

The story of Ruth and Boaz, referred to by the Spirit of God as examples for us, is recorded in the book of Ruth, Chapters 1-4. Ruth was from the Moabite tribe, which had come from the union between Lot and his older daughter. (Genesis 19:36-38). As for Boaz, he was a wealthy landowner in Bethlehem and a kinsman of Elimelech, Naomi's late husband. Naomi was the widow of Elimelech and mother-in-law to Ruth. Ruth's husband had died and she had decided to stay with her mother-in-law.

It was while Ruth was gleaning in Boaz' fields that Boaz noticed her. Her mother-in-law was very instrumental in preparing her and causing favour to fall on her with Boaz because Ruth took instructions from Naomi and obeyed her. In this story we see that two different tribes and nationalities came together irrespective of past experiences or circumstances. Boaz was much older than Ruth but through that union Obed was born. Obed became the father of Jesse and Jesse became the father of King David. Eventually the genealogy reaches Jesus Christ.

At present I do not fully understand why God said we would be like Ruth and Boaz but I believe in time we shall have a full understanding! What I can testify to now is that through our marriage God has broken down cultural barriers, traditions and human customs!

The Proposal

Peter Joseph, my Pastor, proposed to me in April 2008 by going on one knee in front of the entire congregation and I said "Yes!" We were officially courting and still waiting to see what the Lord would do. Both our families were initially hurt because they had not come across such a thing before, so it was like news to them. But once they understood they stood with us in the process. I love them and I do not blame them because they did not understand. Neither did we. My Pastor bought me a beautiful ring as a sign to me that we were officially engaged and as a seal of the new chapter that was beginning in our lives. I was relieved that God's will was coming to pass in front of my eyes.

To God be all the glory, honour and adoration.

A few days after our engagement it was Good Friday and one of the Tele-evangelists we love and respect, Pastor Benny Hinn, was coming from the United States to London ExCel. My Pastor and I decided to attend that conference and took two ladies along with us. We had no clue as to what God had in store for us that day.

Truly those who are led by the Spirit of God are the sons of God. (Rom.8:14) We drove around to find a train station, passing through many stations trying to park our car. We could not find the parking space we wanted since it was a Bank holiday. We could have got a connecting train at Plumstead, Woolwich, and at Maze Hill. But when God has a divine plan He redirects the course of your journey. After many attempts we all decided to drive to Greenwich Railway Station where we found a parking space. We left the car but on our way to the Greenwich docklands light railway my Pastor and husband-to-be realised he had left his Bible in the car. He went back to the car to pick up his Bible. On his way back he saw a white couple who he thought were Jehovah's Witnesses and he thought to himself, "I will witness to them."

As he walked back to them they asked for directions to the ExCel for the Benny Hinn conference. As they were going to the same conference and were also born again Christians, they followed my husband. We later found out that they were Swedish and the wife could speak a bit of English. Because we had gone ahead of my Pastor the three of us were already sitting in the train. The moment the wife Anna Rosberg walked onto the train she pointed at me and said "You are the

Pastor's wife!" I was shocked and so were the other two girls as well as my Pastor. God had done it again, picking me out from the other two ladies! What an accurate God we serve. We cannot hide from the Spirit of God. Wherever we go He is there and we cannot hide from Him.

We later found out that God had sent them for us. In the train they tried to communicate and the wife was interpreting. When we got to ExCel for the Benny Hinn Conference we could not concentrate. It was as if that conference was meant just for Peter Joseph and Evangelist Bernt Rosberg to minister to one another. They prophesied to each other and interpretation was given by the wife throughout the first session.

After that they asked us where our church was and we told them. We invited them to come on the Saturday to Colim Ministries Plumstead. The moment they entered the sanctuary they asked us to call our leaders as they said God had a word for the church. We had two witnesses who came over to the church. They prophesied to my now husband and said "The Lord has given you a wife so you can do the end time work together." That day my Pastor broke down in tears because the Holy Spirit convicted him greatly that all along He was sending confirmation and he had doubted God even when He was the one who had been speaking to him.

God is our present help in time of need, very faithful to fulfil all his promises!

Evangelist Bernt and Anna Rosberg were an answer to our prayer. God sent us Swedish people who reside in Norway to tell us of our destiny and to confirm that I had truly heard God accurately. The other surprise God had in store for us was that for this same couple God had spoken to the woman first just as He had done with me and they are fifteen years apart in age. They were our angels sent to confirm and comfort us. Because of their role in confirming our marriage, God then used them to open doors for my Pastor to preach in Norwegian Bible schools, TV stations and various churches.

After their departure we started planning for our wedding, both a cultural and a church wedding. All things worked together for good in the end.

After their visit we begin to experience supernatural experiences in the church. Angelic spirits came upon people and they began to prophesy that the wedding must be sped up and go ahead. It was as if in that season of 2008 all that God wanted to see was for us to be married and doing His will.

By September 2008 the Ministry was full of different people who believed in us. God sent them to us and God confirmed to them all why He had put my husband and me together. They understood and stood with us in prayers as well as in financial support.

We started preparing for the wedding but we did not have enough money and as a couple we were both worried and concerned about the provision. One day we were driving towards an area called Erith in Kent when a white van appeared in front of us. The van had a picture of two dogs kissing and on it was written "God will provide". This sign made me realise that our marriage was very important to God and that He was willing to show us all the signs to make sure that we went ahead with it.

We also went through some Marriage Counselling sessions with Bishop Jos Brissette from New Rivers of Life Ministries. He spent time sharing insights and testimonies about marriage. In November 2008 my husband gave a dowry to my parents in appreciation of me and of the family I was coming from. That day we had an awesome family reunion. Then after what seemed a long and gruelling but learning process our wedding day arrived.

Our Wedding Day

On the 13 December 2008 I woke up full of joy and peace. It was raining heavily and the opportune time to sing "Showers of Blessing", a wedding song. I wore this beautiful gown and Oh! God's glory was all over me! I had lost so much weight but I was still in good shape.

At the same time my husband was preparing alongside his groomsmen. I was pampered and cared for by my Aunties, Pee, Rose and Carol and a spiritual mother at that time, Mother Joyce, who helped me with all the finishing touches. I thank God also for my young brother and presently Youth Pastor in our church, Reverend Louis Benhura who had done my make up with the help of our friend Yinka Williams.

What pleased me more was everyone in both our families was happy for us and wished to spoil us. A Rolls Royce came for me and my Best Girl, Aunt Marjorie, and my brother, Reverend Louis, who represented my father on that day.

We were chauffer-driven to Greenwich South Baptist Church where 200 people turned out from all walks of life. The majority of those who attended were Pastors and Ministers of the gospel from all over England. Evangelist Bernt Rosberg and his wife Anna came from Norway to seal what God had revealed to both of them concerning our marriage.

My bridal teamed arrived earlier before me in their Limousine and had walked on the aisle with the special song my husband and I chose, "Our God is an awesome God, He reigns from heaven above with wisdom, power and love Our God is an awesome God! It was the Donnie Mc Clurkin version, which ministers to my Spirit so much. When we also arrived at the church mats were laid for us to walk on. In Zimbabwean culture women especially on their wedding day tend not walk on the bare ground. What I observed from the many weddings I attended for years is that, usually the family of the groom will put down cloths and mats for the bride to walk on until they get to the aisle. As the Bride walks in the Church they Will be singing and ululating as the Groom's family will be excited to be gaining a daughter in law. Sometimes there is teasing that goes on and if one is sensitive you might get offended, but truly it is done for fun. In my case because my husband is from Grenada, we had to do things slightly differently to accommodate him and my new family. My side of the family laid mats for me instead, from the Rolls Royce we were in to the church entrance.

My brother, Reverend Louis, held my hand all the way to the altar, whilst Pastor Caroline Joseph sang "Let the Bride say come, Let the Bride say come, Let the Bride of the Lord say Come Lord Jesus".

Meanwhile Bishop Jos who was officiating the wedding was waiting with a big smile on his face to welcome us.

I will not forget the moment when I walked into the church and my husband was even too shy to look at me. It was only when we were both called to come up to the rostrum to exchange our vows when He boldly looked at me.

I also remember that before the wedding the Spirit of God had given us specific instructions on how the wedding was to be conducted. God had really shown his manifest presence in so many ways. The Lord told us He would visit us at the wedding. God surprised us yet again, when during the ceremony a man walked in wearing something like a Jewish rabbi's outfit, accompanied by our friend, Prophet Rev Richard Mitchell, who was preaching the sermon for the wedding. During the time for prayer the man dressed in Jewish clothes began to prophesy and he covered us with a talith or a prayer shawl and prophesied that Yeshua Hamashiach (which means Jesus the Messiah in Hebrew) had sent him to us. The moment my husband heard this he broke down in tears and remembered what the Spirit of God had said.

Our wedding party ended up with a Jewish theme and we were given sacred oils from Israel and also had a Jewish dance too. God really made us feel special in front of our family, friends and even some of our critics. Truly God is a rewarder of those who diligently seek him.

I mentioned earlier on, in the chapter about my Life in the United Kingdom, that God later had a surprise for me. The surprise was, when my husband and I went for our honeymoon to come together as husband and wife after our wedding party, I found out I was totally restored of my womanhood just like a new born baby girl. Science cannot explain this but it is called a 'miracle'. There is blessing for obedience. The obedience was when I had rededicated my life to Jesus I had never again involved my self in ungodly relationships. It took God a period of three years exactly to do the cleansing and purification work on my body. I praise God for his continual love for me !!!

EPILOGUE
Ruth and Boaz 7 Years Later

We are married nearly seven years now on 13 December this year of our Lord, 2015. We give God thanks for holding our marriage together. It has truly been a great journey of getting to know each other more. The pain and rejection we went through waiting for confirmation of the marriage was worth it. Now we see the blessings, thank you God. We go through all the things that other married people go through but we both know we have a 'Big' God on our side and our lovely families who are very supportive.

As a couple from mixed cultures, it brings such flavour. We never run out of ideas what to cook as we both have different staple diets. My husband being Grenadan, taught me how to cook different dishes from his home country from the time we got married. I also cook Zimbabwean food and both of us eat and enjoy together.

Being in a mixed marriage comes with some challenges as well. We have age difference to consider and also different upbringing. I honestly have to say that we both have had to relearn things afresh so we can meet half way. Being in a mixed culture marriage, one can easily feel that their ways of doing things where they come from, is better than the other. Thank God for the word of God that renews our mind daily from such thinking.

It is important that this book reveals the truth about our marriage, so that some people will not be deceived by thinking that when God put a couple together everything will fall in line straight away. Dear readers, no one is perfect as yet we are all work in progress! God will continue to totally refine us so we are more like Him.

Great doors have opened for us as well since we got married, because we obeyed God. We even had a great opportunity to be on 'Believe TV', a Christian television station here in the United Kingdom. For three years we were on it preaching to nations! Thanks be to Jesus and all the Pastors He has used to help us! We thank God for Reverend Ezekiel Thompson and Pastor Alex Omokudu for introducing us to the TV Ministry and helping us to be established in the media arena. We preach and minister locally and overseas as a couple.

Two years ago my husband was consecrated as a Bishop in the Trans Atlantic and Pacific Alliance of Churches. Truly God has been good to us.

We thank God for Archbishop JP and his wife Bishop Sodnaia Hackman who are our spiritual parents and covering. I was also ordained a Reverend at the same time. God has done so much for us in a short time that we will never cease to give Him praise. Bishop and I, have ministered and prophesied to many Saints over the years in conferences and it is all the Lord's doing. Many of the prophecies that my husband and I have given to people over the years have now come to pass. We are grateful to God for this special gift. This year I even had the privilege of travelling to six nations including stop-overs and graduating from Bible College for the second time. It was all the doing of the Lord, and God has just remained faithful throughout!

We are overseeing COLIM Ministries in England and Norway and we thank God for the lovely sons and daughters and ministers He has sent our way! The most important thing is that we love each other and we are still together seven years on. God has proven to us that He speaks, He confirms and all his plans concerning our destiny are being manifested. God has proved to us that His Word will not return to him void as (Isa.55:11) says, *"until It shall accomplish what God pleases."*

Our marriage was orchestrated in heaven but we have a great part to play to make sure we stay in God's will. Our joy and hope as a couple is based on a Scripture we have both fallen in love with and with which I conclude this book, (Philiphians 1 : 6), *"Being confident of this very thing, that He who has begun a good work in you will complete it until the day of Jesus Christ."* (Philippians 1:6)

"Finish Lord what you started in us in Jesus' name!" AMEN AND AMEN

*At home with my brother, my cousin and my aunties getting ready
to leave for the church ceremony*

*My husband and his best man Pastor Isaac Attram patiently waiting
for me to come inside the church*

Arriving at Greenwich South Baptist Church with Evangelist Pat Bennet and my brother Louis

My brother Louis walking me up the aisle representing the father of the bride

Standing alongside my husband-to-be

Pastor Caroline Joseph singing at our wedding

Church venue

Exchange of rings with our officiating Minister, Bishop Jos Brissette

Surprise guest Prophet Steve, sent by God with a message

Ministers of the Gospel sealing our marriage in prayer

My groom looking a bit teary because of God's faithfulness

Signing the marriage register

*Our witnesses Marjorie Benhura and Pastor Isaac Mac Attram
join us as we sign the register*

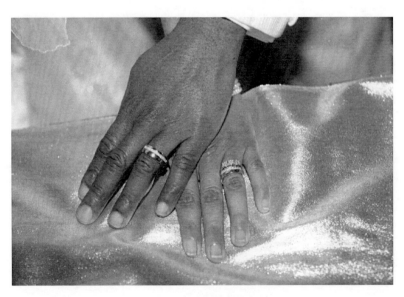

Our wedding rings

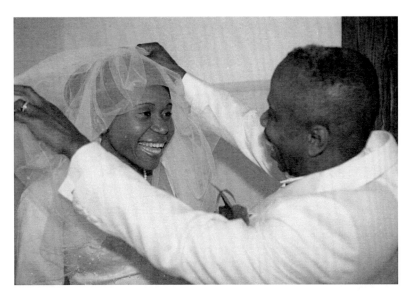

My husband removing my veil

Kissing the bride

Coming out of ceremony as Mr and Mrs Joseph

*Our officiating Ministers Rev Richard Mitchell on the left
and Bishop Jos Brissette and Prophet Steve*

My side of the family

My husband's side of the family

Our bridesmaids

Our grooms men

The New Rivers of Life Ministry and Bethel team

With Rev H Laing with his family and friends

With Pastor David Midzi and LfT

The female bridal crew

My mini bridal team

Evangelist Bernt Rosberg praying for us

In the venue dancing with my brother

At the bridal table

Our wedding cake

The Jewish dance

The first dance

Ruth and Boaz of the 21st Century